Weekly & Monthly Planner

Contacts

name ....

address ....

phone ....

email ....

❀ ❀ ❀ ❀ ❀ ❀ ❀

name ....

address ....

phone ....

email ....

❀ ❀ ❀ ❀ ❀ ❀ ❀

name ....

address ....

phone ....

email ....

❀ ❀ ❀ ❀ ❀ ❀ ❀

name ....

address ....

phone ....

email ....

❀ ❀ ❀ ❀ ❀ ❀ ❀

name ....

address ....

phone ....

email ....

❀ ❀ ❀ ❀ ❀ ❀ ❀

name ....

address ....

phone ....

email ....

Contacts

name ....

address ....

phone ....

email ....

❀   ❀   ❀   ❀   ❀   ❀   ❀

name ....

address ....

phone ....

email ....

❀   ❀   ❀   ❀   ❀   ❀   ❀

name ....

address ....

phone ....

email ....

❀   ❀   ❀   ❀   ❀   ❀   ❀

name ....

address ....

phone ....

email ....

❀   ❀   ❀   ❀   ❀   ❀   ❀

name ....

address ....

phone ....

email ....

❀   ❀   ❀   ❀   ❀   ❀   ❀

name ....

address ....

phone ....

email ....

Contacts

name

address

phone

email

❀ ❀ ❀ ❀ ❀ ❀ ❀

name

address

phone

email

❀ ❀ ❀ ❀ ❀ ❀ ❀

name

address

phone

email

❀ ❀ ❀ ❀ ❀ ❀ ❀

name

address

phone

email

❀ ❀ ❀ ❀ ❀ ❀ ❀

name

address

phone

email

❀ ❀ ❀ ❀ ❀ ❀ ❀

name

address

phone

email

Calendar

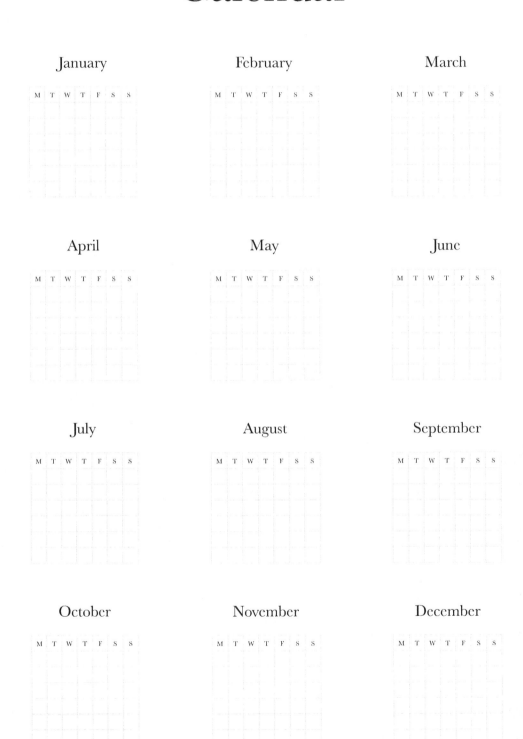

January
M T W T F S S

February
M T W T F S S

March
M T W T F S S

April
M T W T F S S

May
M T W T F S S

June
M T W T F S S

July
M T W T F S S

August
M T W T F S S

September
M T W T F S S

October
M T W T F S S

November
M T W T F S S

December
M T W T F S S

Calendar

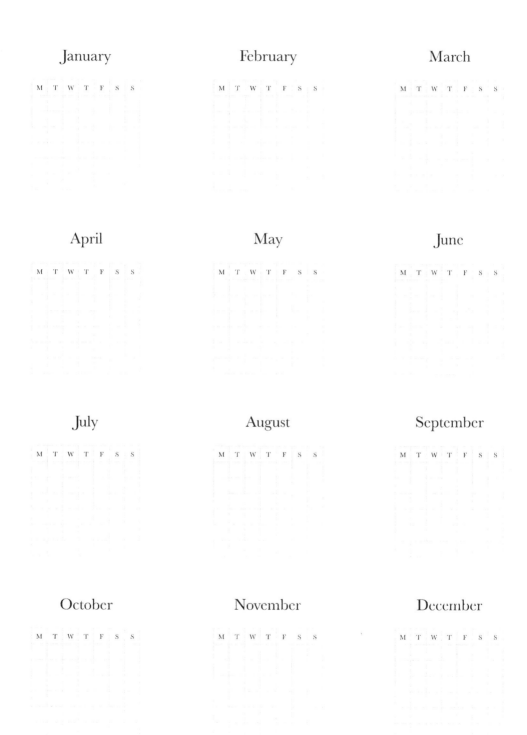

January	February	March
M T W T F S S	M T W T F S S	M T W T F S S

April	May	June
M T W T F S S	M T W T F S S	M T W T F S S

July	August	September
M T W T F S S	M T W T F S S	M T W T F S S

October	November	December
M T W T F S S	M T W T F S S	M T W T F S S

Week

priorities

events | appointments | due dates

notes | ideas

accomplishments

Monday

Tuesday

Wednesday

Thursday

Friday

Saturday

Sunday

Week

priorities

events | appointments | due dates

notes | ideas

accomplishments

Monday

Tuesday

Wednesday

Thursday

Friday

Saturday

Sunday

Week

priorities

events | appointments | due dates

notes | ideas

accomplishments

Monday

Tuesday

Wednesday

Thursday

Friday

Saturday

Sunday

Week

priorities

events | appointments | due dates

notes | ideas

accomplishments

Monday

Tuesday

Wednesday

Thursday

Friday

Saturday

Sunday

Week

priorities

events | appointments | due dates

notes | ideas

accomplishments

Monday

Tuesday

Wednesday

Thursday

Friday

Saturday

Sunday

Week ....

priorities

....

....

....

....

....

....

....

....

....

....

events | appointments | due dates

....

....

....

....

....

....

....

....

....

....

....

....

....

....

....

notes | ideas

accomplishments

....

....

....

....

....

....

....

Monday

Tuesday

Wednesday

Thursday

Friday

Saturday

Sunday

Week

priorities

events | appointments | due dates

notes | ideas

accomplishments

Monday

Tuesday

Wednesday

Thursday

Friday

Saturday

Sunday

Week

priorities

events | appointments | due dates

notes | ideas

accomplishments

Monday

Tuesday

Wednesday

Thursday

Friday

Saturday

Sunday

Week

priorities

events | appointments | due dates

notes | ideas

accomplishments

Monday

Tuesday

Wednesday

Thursday

Friday

Saturday

Sunday

Week

priorities

events | appointments | due dates

notes | ideas

accomplishments

Monday

Tuesday

Wednesday

Thursday

Friday

Saturday

Sunday

Week ....

priorities

events | appointments | due dates

notes | ideas

accomplishments

Monday

Tuesday

Wednesday

Thursday

Friday

Saturday

Sunday

Week

priorities

events | appointments | due dates

notes | ideas

accomplishments

Monday

Tuesday

Wednesday

Thursday

Friday

Saturday

Sunday

Week

priorities

events | appointments | due dates

notes | ideas

accomplishments

Monday

Tuesday

Wednesday

Thursday

Friday

Saturday

Sunday

Week

priorities

events | appointments | due dates

notes | ideas

accomplishments

Monday

Tuesday

Wednesday

Thursday

Friday

Saturday

Sunday

Week

priorities

events | appointments | due dates

notes | ideas

accomplishments

Monday

Tuesday

Wednesday

Thursday

Friday

Saturday

Sunday

Week

priorities

events | appointments | due dates

notes | ideas

accomplishments

Monday

Tuesday

Wednesday

Thursday

Friday

Saturday

Sunday

Week

priorities

events | appointments | due dates

notes | ideas

accomplishments

Monday

Tuesday

Wednesday

Thursday

Friday

Saturday

Sunday

Week

priorities

events | appointments | due dates

notes | ideas

accomplishments

Monday

Tuesday

Wednesday

Thursday

Friday

Saturday

Sunday

Week

priorities

events | appointments | due dates

notes | ideas

accomplishments

Monday

Tuesday

Wednesday

Thursday

Friday

Saturday

Sunday

Week

priorities

events | appointments | due dates

notes | ideas

accomplishments

Monday

Tuesday

Wednesday

Thursday

Friday

Saturday

Sunday

Week

priorities

events | appointments | due dates

notes | ideas

accomplishments

Monday

Tuesday

Wednesday

Thursday

Friday

Saturday

Sunday

Week

priorities

events | appointments | due dates

notes | ideas

accomplishments

Monday

Tuesday

Wednesday

Thursday

Friday

Saturday

Sunday

Week

priorities

events | appointments | due dates

notes | ideas

accomplishments

Monday

Tuesday

Wednesday

Thursday

Friday

Saturday

Sunday

Week ....

priorities

events | appointments | due dates

....

....

....

....

....

....

....

....

....

notes | ideas

accomplishments

Monday

Tuesday

Wednesday

Thursday

Friday

Saturday

Sunday

Week

priorities

events | appointments | due dates

notes | ideas

accomplishments

Monday

Tuesday

Wednesday

Thursday

Friday

Saturday

Sunday

Week

priorities

events | appointments | due dates

notes | ideas

accomplishments

Monday

Tuesday

Wednesday

Thursday

Friday

Saturday

Sunday

Week

priorities

events | appointments | due dates

notes | ideas

accomplishments

Monday

Tuesday

Wednesday

Thursday

Friday

Saturday

Sunday

Week

priorities

events | appointments | due dates

notes | ideas

accomplishments

Monday

Tuesday

Wednesday

Thursday

Friday

Saturday

Sunday

Week

priorities

events | appointments | due dates

notes | ideas

accomplishments

Monday

Tuesday

Wednesday

Thursday

Friday

Saturday

Sunday

Week

priorities

events | appointments | due dates

notes | ideas

accomplishments

Monday

Tuesday

Wednesday

Thursday

Friday

Saturday

Sunday

Week

priorities

events | appointments | due dates

notes | ideas

accomplishments

Monday

Tuesday

Wednesday

Thursday

Friday

Saturday

Sunday

Week

priorities

events | appointments | due dates

notes | ideas

accomplishments

Monday

Tuesday

Wednesday

Thursday

Friday

Saturday

Sunday

Week

priorities

events | appointments | due dates

notes | ideas

accomplishments

Monday

Tuesday

Wednesday

Thursday

Friday

Saturday

Sunday

Week

priorities

events | appointments | due dates

notes | ideas

accomplishments

Monday

Tuesday

Wednesday

Thursday

Friday

Saturday

Sunday

Week

priorities

events | appointments | due dates

notes | ideas

accomplishments

Monday

Tuesday

Wednesday

Thursday

Friday

Saturday

Sunday

Week

priorities

events | appointments | due dates

notes | ideas

accomplishments

Monday

Tuesday

Wednesday

Thursday

Friday

Saturday

Sunday

Week

priorities

events | appointments | due dates

notes | ideas

accomplishments

Monday

Tuesday

Wednesday

Thursday

Friday

Saturday

Sunday

Week

priorities

events | appointments | due dates

notes | ideas

accomplishments

Monday

Tuesday

Wednesday

Thursday

Friday

Saturday

Sunday

Week

priorities

events | appointments | due dates

notes | ideas

accomplishments

Monday

Tuesday

Wednesday

Thursday

Friday

Saturday

Sunday

Week

priorities

events | appointments | due dates

notes | ideas

accomplishments

Monday

Tuesday

Wednesday

Thursday

Friday

Saturday

Sunday

Week

priorities

events | appointments | due dates

notes | ideas

accomplishments

Monday

Tuesday

Wednesday

Thursday

Friday

Saturday

Sunday

Week

priorities

events | appointments | due dates

notes | ideas

accomplishments

Monday

Tuesday

Wednesday

Thursday

Friday

Saturday

Sunday

Week

priorities

events | appointments | due dates

notes | ideas

accomplishments

Monday

Tuesday

Wednesday

Thursday

Friday

Saturday

Sunday

Week

priorities

events | appointments | due dates

notes | ideas

accomplishments

Monday

Tuesday

Wednesday

Thursday

Friday

Saturday

Sunday

Week

priorities

events | appointments | due dates

notes | ideas

accomplishments

Monday

Tuesday

Wednesday

Thursday

Friday

Saturday

Sunday

Week

priorities

events | appointments | due dates

notes | ideas

accomplishments

Monday

Tuesday

Wednesday

Thursday

Friday

Saturday

Sunday

Week

priorities

events | appointments | due dates

notes | ideas

accomplishments

Monday

Tuesday

Wednesday

Thursday

Friday

Saturday

Sunday

Week

priorities

events | appointments | due dates

notes | ideas

accomplishments

Monday

Tuesday

Wednesday

Thursday

Friday

Saturday

Sunday

Week

priorities

notes | ideas

accomplishments

Monday

Tuesday

Wednesday

Thursday

Friday

Saturday

Sunday

Week

priorities

events | appointments | due dates

notes | ideas

accomplishments

Monday

Tuesday

Wednesday

Thursday

Friday

Saturday

Sunday

Week

priorities

events | appointments | due dates

notes | ideas

accomplishments

Monday

Tuesday

Wednesday

Thursday

Friday

Saturday

Sunday

Week

priorities

events | appointments | due dates

notes | ideas

accomplishments

Monday

Tuesday

Wednesday

Thursday

Friday

Saturday

Sunday

Week

priorities

events | appointments | due dates

notes | ideas

accomplishments

Monday

Tuesday

Wednesday

Thursday

Friday

Saturday

Sunday

Week

priorities

events | appointments | due dates

notes | ideas

accomplishments

Monday

Tuesday

Wednesday

Thursday

Friday

Saturday

Sunday

Week

priorities

events | appointments | due dates

notes | ideas

accomplishments

Monday

Tuesday

Wednesday

Thursday

Friday

Saturday

Sunday

notes

notes

notes